AF406131

UNDERSTANDING SALVATION

George Ngondo

First Edition

BOOK HOUSE Publishers

Understanding Salvation

First Edition Copyright ©2017

Unless otherwise stated, all scriptures are taken from:

1. KJV - King James Version
2. NIV – New International Version
3. NASB – New American Standard Bible

The publishers aim is to produce books that will help bring revival in the lives of Christians for the purposes of building them up into functional Christians in the kingdom of God. The views expressed herein are inspired by the Holy Spirit and we expect readers to ask the Holy Spirit for guidance as they read with reference to the word of God.

ISBN: 978-9966-100-90-0

Contents

This book is dedicated to the Almighty God for His grace upon my life and for continuously teaching me.

Forward

After man lost his fellowship with his first love at the Garden of Eden, God in His unending mercies decided to restore this fellowship with man by sending his only begotten son, Jesus Christ, to redeem mankind back to Himself through death at the cross at Calvary.

Through the shed blood of Jesus at Calvary, Man's sins were atoned and it is those who look up to Calvary, whose sins are forgiven.

This book brings a new understanding to salvation and purpose and subsequently links salvation to purpose. It lays bare the will of God towards man as regards salvation with the aim of bringing man to experience the fullness of salvation.

This book reveals and defines the meaning of God's Glory in an astounding way. The book also acknowledges that many born again Christians are yet to experience the full joy of salvation (the Glory of God) which is hidden in discovering their purpose in the Kingdom of God.

The writer outlines that salvation is the first step among a series of steps which build up towards restoration of God's Glory upon a man's life.

This book has been written at a time when born again Christians are experiencing a disconnect from God and are groping in the dark trying to know God's will and purpose for their lives.

The book is an easy read and it is my hope that as you read this book, it will prepare you for the great revival that is about to be poured and experienced by the saints who are eagerly waiting for the day of the Lord.

Grace Christian Fellowship - Nairobi

INTRODUCTION

Salvation has been widely misunderstood. Many people today say that they are saved, but do not have the basic understanding of what salvation really means. In this book, I have penned down an understanding of salvation the way it has been revealed to me by the Holy Spirit.

I want to thank the Lord God Almighty for guidance in compiling this book. I also want to give thanks to my Lord Jesus Christ because it is by him that I am saved and to the Holy Spirit for administering to me this gift of writing.

It is my sincere hope that you will be greatly blessed and enriched as you read through this book as you work on your salvation to discover your purpose and limitless potential in the Kingdom of God.

CHAPTER 1

The Beginning

1.1: Understanding the Creation and Formation of Man

To understand salvation, it is important to understand the beginning of man.

Genesis chapter 1 outlines the creations of God. On the First Day, God created light, on the second day He created Firmament, on the third day he created dry ground, on the fourth day he created the Sun, the Moon and the stars, on the fifth day he created the fish and birds and on the sixth day He created living creatures on the land - cattle, and creeping things, beast of the earth each after its kind. On the sixth day God **created** man.

(Genesis 1: 26 -27)

<u>26</u> *And God said, Let us make man in our image, after our likeness: and let them have dominion over the fish of the sea, and over the fowl of the air, and over the cattle, and over all the earth, and over every creeping thing that creepeth upon the earth.*

<u>27</u> *So God **created man** in **his own image**, in the image of God created he him; male and female created he them.*

(Genesis 2: 5-8)

*5 And every plant of the field before it was in the earth, and every herb of the field before it grew: for the LORD God had not caused it to rain upon the earth, **and there was not a man to till the ground**.*

6 But there went up a mist from the earth, and watered the whole face of the ground.

*7 And the **LORD God formed man** of the dust of the ground, and breathed into his nostrils the breath of life; and man became a living soul.*

8 And the LORD God planted a garden eastward in Eden; and there he put the man whom he had formed.

These scriptures give us a clear revelation that man was *first created* before *he was formed*. Before man walked the earth, he existed in the image of God. God is spirit; therefore man existed as a spirit being - the image of God - before he was formed.

This is further confirmed in Jeremiah 1: 5 when God told Jeremiah … *"Before I **formed** you in the womb I knew you, before you were born I set you apart; I appointed you as a prophet to the nations."*

For God to know Jeremiah before He formed him, it means that Jeremiah existed. This is a confirmation that before God formed you in your mother's womb; you existed as a spirit being.

It is only God who knows how long you existed as a spirit being before He formed you in your mother's womb!

The character of God is such that He does not do anything without a purpose. Therefore, Just like He told Jeremiah that he had appointed or ordained him as a prophet to the nations before he formed him, the same applies to you! You were formed for a purpose.

Jesus also showed us clearly in Hebrews 10:5-7 that when God puts you here on earth, he has a purpose for you. This is what he said:

*<u>5</u> Therefore, when Christ came into the world, he said: "Sacrifice and offering you did not desire, **but a body you prepared for me**; <u>6</u> with burnt offerings and sin offerings you were not pleased. <u>7</u> Then I said, 'Here I am—it is written about me in the scroll—I have come to do your will, my God.' "*

Note what Jesus says here - *"But a body you prepared for me"*…A womb was made available (Mary's) to carry Jesus or to *form* him and deliver him into the world to fulfill a purpose. Jesus existed before he was sent to the world.

Can you begin to see that you also existed before God formed you in the womb of your mother to fulfill a purpose?

The purpose of Jeremiah was to be a prophet to the nations.

The purpose of Jesus is outlined in Luke 4:18-19

<u>18</u> "The Spirit of the Lord is on me, because he has anointed me to proclaim good news to the poor. He has sent me to proclaim freedom for the prisoners and recovery of sight for the blind, to set the oppressed free, <u>19</u> to proclaim the year of the Lord's favor."

This was a fulfillment of what was written about him in and in Isaiah 61: 1-3.

Your purpose is _______________________________________

It is my prayer that at the end of this book God will begin to reveal to you your purpose here on earth and come back and fill this blank.

1.2: The Fellowship of Adam and God

Now, after Adam was formed out of dust, he was put in the Garden of Eden which God had planted and was commanded to eat from all the fruits of the garden except from the tree of the knowledge of good and evil.

(Genesis 2:16 -17)

<u>16</u> And the LORD God commanded the man, saying, of every tree of the garden thou mayest freely eat:
<u>17</u> But of the tree of the knowledge of good and evil, thou shalt not eat of it: for in the day that thou eatest thereof thou shalt surely die.

Genesis chapter 3 gives us an indication of how God used to visit Adam in the Garden of Eden to have fellowship or companionship with him. Even though Adam was formed out of dust, he still had the image of God in him. God delighted to have fellowship with Adam. God created man so that he could enjoy a close relationship with him - the father and child kind of relationship.

Genesis Chapter 3 outlines 4 things:

1. The deception by the serpent (Verse 1 - 7),

2. God Charges Adam and Eve (Verse 8 - 15)

3. The Punishment to Mankind (Verse 9 – 20)

4. The Expulsion from Paradise (Verse 21 – 24)

After the deception by the serpent at the Garden of Eden, Adam and his wife Eve sinned and lost the close relationship or fellowship they had with God. Sin Separates man from God.

What kind of fellowship was this?
It is clear that Adam enjoyed a close fellowship with God at the Garden of Eden before he was expelled. In trying to understand this fellowship, we must first agree that:
1. There can be no fellowship without communication and
2. There can be no communication without a language.

Fellowship can be defined as a friendly association, especially with someone whom you share something in common or same interests.

Fellowship can either be physical or non-physical. A physical fellowship happens when you are in the presence of another person; you can see each other and even have verbal communication.

On the other hand, non-physical fellowship happens when you are not in the presence of a person but you can feel them and you even have a hunch on what they may be going through. This happens when there is a spiritual connection. For example have you ever called someone and the first thing they say is…I was thinking about you before you called. Your spiritual antennas were on the same wavelength that is why you could feel them and decided to call them.

Non-physical fellowship is always very strong in a mother and child relationship. A mother can tell when her baby is not well and will take appropriate action like consulting a physician etc.

In both physical and no-physical fellowships, communication takes place. In physical fellowships we mostly communicate verbally. In non-physical fellowships we communicate mostly through what is called discernment.

Did God have a physical or non-physical fellowship with Adam? To answer this question, let us take a look at Genesis 3: 8-10

*<u>8</u> And they **heard the voice of the LORD God** walking in the garden in the cool of the day: and Adam and his wife **hid** themselves from the **presence** of the LORD God amongst the trees of the garden. <u>9</u> And the LORD God called unto Adam, and said unto him, Where art thou? <u>10</u> And he said, I heard thy voice in the garden, and I was afraid, because I was naked; and I hid myself.*

Adam and eve hid themselves from the presence of God when they heard Him approaching. You can only hide from someone you can see.

This could mean that at the Garden of Eden Adam and Eve enjoyed both physical (Visible Presence) and non-physical (when God was physically absent) fellowship with God. You may ask? But God is spirit, how could He be seen by Adam and Eve?

God is able to take a physical form of either a man or whatever He chooses. We know that in Genesis 18, God appears as one of the three (seemingly human) visitors to Abraham. It is possible that God took the form of a man whenever he visited Adam and Eve.

In this physical presence, God spoke to Adam and Eve in a language that they both understood clearly. For it to be recorded as *"they heard the voice of God"* means that it was audible to them.

Question - what happened to this audible language that God used to communicate with Adam and Eve? Was it lost to human kind? Are we able to re-learn this language?

The answers to these questions will become clearer when you understand the purpose of salvation in the following chapters. However, the flipside of this is that this language became lost to mankind over the generations after Adam was expelled from the presence of God.

For a language to be preserved, the originator (which in this case is God himself) and the descendants must continue to engage in it. There are several reported cases of languages of men that have become extinct as a result of detachment from the origin. Having been detached from their creator, the original language between man and God faded into oblivion and subsequently the fellowship between man and God was lost.

Fellowship and Prosperity

God designed man to be connected to Him through fellowship for man to flourish. Outside this fellowship, man cannot thrive or prosper.

The prosperity (all round wellness) of man is dependent on man being connected to God through fellowship.

God's + Man's fellowship = Man's Prosperity

God loves fellowship. His Trinity attests to this. Before He created man, God had fellowship with himself – God the father, God the son and God the Holy Spirit. That is why before he created man he conferred with the Trinity… *"Let **us** make man in our image."*

In a similar fashion, man, was also created to be a creature of fellowship. Man was supposed to fellowship with his first love – God. The fellowship with God is supposed to cause man to prosper.

Psalm 35:27 *"Let them shout for joy, and be glad, that favour my righteous cause: yea, let them say continually, Let the LORD be magnified, which **hath pleasure in the prosperity** of his servant."*

The psalmist here seems to be saying that those who delight in God's righteous cause (share the same interests with God) will shout for joy and be glad as they prosper. Remember fellowshipping is the friendly association with someone whom you share same interests.

After man sinned at the Garden of Eden, he lost his fellowship with his first love. Ever since, because man carries the DNA of God, his heart has been constantly looking for something to replace God's fellowship. Outside God's fellowship man can only exist but cannot prosper. In other words, man cannot have wellness or joy or gladness of heart.

Therefore man outside God's fellowship is lost and will not thrive. He needs help to be restored back to this former fellowship with God so that he may begin to prosper again.

The following is a diagrammatic demonstration of God's fellowship with man.

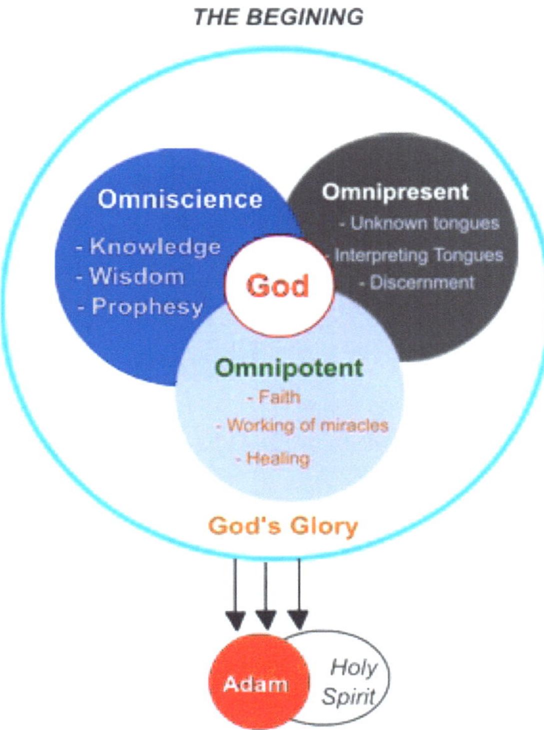

The diagram shows the 3 sides of God:

Omniscience:

All knowing (Knowledgeable, Wise, Prophesy)
All Knowledge comes from God, God is wise (Proverbs 3:19), and Prophesy means that he knows the beginning and the end.

Omnipresent:

Ever present (Unknown Tongues, interpreting tongues, discernment). All languages originated from God. Unknown tongues (1 Corinthians 14:2) - is the language between God and man.

God gives man enablement to interpret tongues.

God gives man discernment. Discernment is a non-verbal language that is used to communicate in the spirit realm.

All these elements represent language. Language is the vehicle of communication and because God is ever present, man needs these elements to fellowship with God.

Omnipotent:

All powerful (faith, working of miracles, healing)

Faith is the currency in the spirit realm. You can access anything in heaven through faith. Without faith it is impossible to please God. (Hebrews 11:6).

Faith, working of miracles and healing are gifts of the Holy Spirit (1 Corinthians 12:9-10) and show cases God's power.

All these components (Omniscience, Omnipresent, and Omnipotent) represent the Glory of God.

If you have noticed, within these three components of God's Glory, are the elements of the gifts of the Holy Spirit. (1 Corinthians 12:7-11).

*7 Now to each one the manifestation of the Spirit is given for the common good. 8 To one there is given through the Spirit a message of **wisdom**, to another a message of **knowledge** by means of the same Spirit, 9 to another **faith** by the same Spirit, to another **gifts of healing** by that one Spirit, 10 to another **miraculous powers**, to another **prophecy**, to another **distinguishing between spirits (discernment)**, to another speaking in **different kinds of tongues**, and to still another the **interpretation of tongues**. 11 All these are the work of one and the same Spirit, and he distributes them to each one, just as he determines.*

God's Glory is apparently the illumination these nine elements (gifts of the Holy Spirit) upon a man's life.

If these nine elements are illuminated upon your life, you will prosper, and men will see the Glory of the Lord upon your life.

When Adam sinned, he was separated from the Glory of God and these elements became absent in his life as seen in the diagram below:

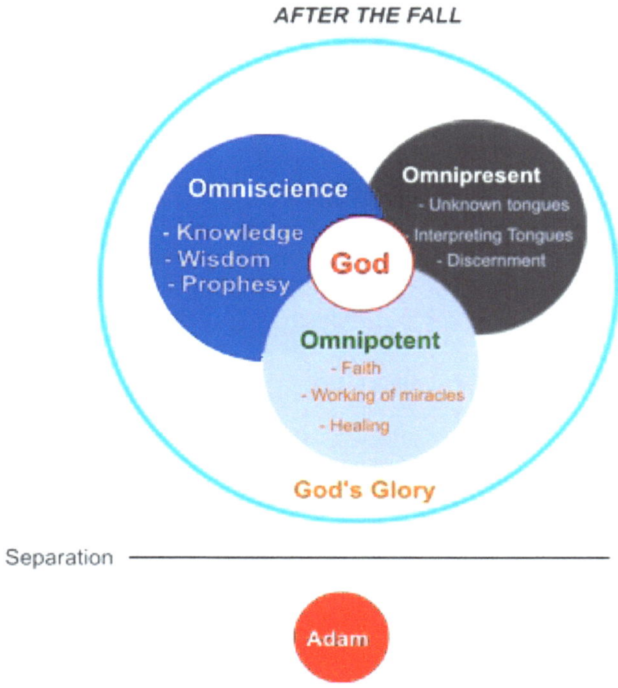

The fall meant a separation from God's Glory. From that time all these components of God's Glory were removed from a man's life, man began to fall ill, his understanding became futile, and he lost the ability to communicate in the spirit realm. Even though man continued to live, he could not prosper because the Glory that causes him to prosper was no more.

Therefore, fellowshipping with God ensures prosperity through His glory which is ever present in your life as represented by the nine gifts of the Holy Spirit.

Therefore, it is clear that the fall of man took away prosperity from man. Prosperity means: to be well physically (without illness), to be well spiritually (in constant communion with God) and to be well intellectually (having Godly Knowledge and wisdom).

Summary

- God created man to have fellowship with him.
- Outside God's fellowship, man will only exist but cannot prosper. Fellowship with God brings prosperity to man.
- The Glory of God is made up of three components (Omnipresent, Omniscience and Omnipotent) which contain nine elements (Knowledge, wisdom, prophesy, unknown tongues, interpreting of tongues, Discernment, Faith, working of miracles and healing) which are the gifts of the Holy Spirit.
- When we say all Glory and Honor belongs to God, we actually acknowledge the presence of these components in Him – this is worship.

With this understanding of the beginning and the purpose of God for man, the next section reveals why salvation is the gift from God to restore this fellowship and subsequently give you access to the former Glory of God - that you may prosper.

CHAPTER 2

Salvation

2.1: What is salvation?

Salvation is the beginning of the restoration of the former fellowship between man and God. Salvation is meant to restore the Glory of God upon a man's life.

Salvation came to the world through the death of Jesus Christ. Remember the purpose of Jesus Christ as outlined in Luke 4:18-19 was to proclaim good news to the poor, to proclaim freedom for the prisoners, recovery of sight for the blind, to set the oppressed free and to proclaim the year of the Lord's favor.

This is simply salvation. Jesus came to bring salvation to the poor, to the prisoners, to the oppressed, to the sick, to the blind and to the world.

Therefore, when you accept Jesus Christ as the Lord over your life, you receive the gift of salvation. You receive salvation when you confess that you are a sinner, acknowledge that Jesus is the son of God, that he died for your sins and rose again and finally ask Jesus to forgive your sin.

Anyone can be saved regardless of their religious or ethnic background on making this confession.

John 3:16 *"For God so loved the world that He gave His one and only Son, that everyone who believes in Him shall not perish but have eternal life."*

Some Christian doctrines teach that anyone practicing the Christian faith is saved. This is not true. Salvation demands that one makes the confession with their mouth.

<u>Romans 10:9-10</u> *if you declare with your mouth, "Jesus is Lord," and believe in your heart that God raised him from the dead, you will be saved. For it is with your heart that you believe and are justified, and it is with your mouth that you profess your faith and are saved.*

Salvation is a gift from God to those who accept Jesus Christ as their Lord.

<u>Ephesians 2: 8-9:</u> *For it is by grace you have been saved, through faith—and this is not from yourselves, it is the gift of God— not by works, so that no one can boast.*

2.2 Salvation is a process

Now, salvation is not a onetime thing. It is a process of renewal to conform to the image of Christ. Philippians 2:12 confirms this. It says... *Therefore, my beloved, just as you have always obeyed, not only in my presence, but now even more in my absence, continue to work out your salvation with fear and trembling.*

What does working out your salvation with fear and trembling mean? It means that salvation is a journey that begins with us confessing Jesus as our Lord and savior and then thereafter, the process of renewal of our ways.

Now, salvation is a three step process. Having seen that man is a triune being consisting of a Spirit, a Soul and a Body; it follows that each of these components will have to go through the process of salvation. The first component of man to experience salvation is the spirit man, followed by the soul and then the body. Here, I explain how each component is affected by salvation.

Step 1: Salvation of Our Spirit.

This happens' the instant we receive Jesus as our Lord and savior. This is what is called being born again. In this first step, our spirit becomes alive. Remember that the spirit man died when Adam and Eve ate the forbidden fruit. God had told Adam in Genesis 2:17…*But of the tree of the knowledge of good and evil, thou shalt not eat of it: for in the day that thou eatest thereof thou shalt surely die.*

This was not a physical death but a spiritual death and when we are born into this world by our parents, we come having inherited this fallen nature. We are spiritually dead. But on receiving salvation, our spirit man becomes alive again, but just like a new born, we are not aware of our spiritual surroundings.

Despite the fact that at new birth, we are not aware of our spiritual surroundings, we have the potential of becoming aware of the spirit realm as we grow through the word of God.

Paul says that: *But because of His great love for us, God, who is rich in mercy, made us alive with Christ, even when we were dead in our trespasses. It is by grace you have been saved!* (*Ephesians 2:4-5*)

When you receive Christ, you are made alive with him and it is by the grace of God.

Step 2: Salvation of Our Soul

Our soul is the component of man that consists of: Our Mind, Our Emotions and Our Intellect. After the death of the spirit man in the Garden of Eden, our soul took over the running of man. Our soul is also referred to variously as the flesh in the scriptures. Before our salvation, our soul is the part of man that is schooled in the ways of this world. It is the seat of all self-centeredness of man: Greed, strife, adultery, contentions etc. Our soul looks at things from the perspective of: what will I get in this? In God's eyes, our soul is totally corrupt because on in its own, it cannot acknowledge God or even comprehend that there is parent spiritual realm.

The salvation of our soul takes the longest and encompasses our entire journey in this world after we get born again. The salvation of our soul involves unlearning the things of this of this world and replacing them with spiritual truths.

This salvation is referred to in Romans 12:2 which says…*And be not conformed to this world: but be ye transformed by the renewing of your mind, that ye may prove what is that good, and acceptable, and perfect, will of God.*

The entry of the word of God brings about this transformation. Jesus praying for the disciples, said in John 17:17: *They are not of the world, just as I am not of the world. Sanctify them by the truth; Your word is truth.*

The renewing of the mind, which is part of our soul, is accomplished by the sanctifying or cleansing power of the word of truth or the word God.

When we finally bow out of this world or transition out of this age into eternity upon our death, the only thing that we take into eternity is our character. Our soul is responsible for our character. A Godly character is described in Galatians 5:22 and includes… love, joy, peace, longsuffering, gentleness, goodness, faith, meekness, and temperance.

Step 3: Salvation of Our Body

Salvation is not complete until our body is saved. The sin that Adam and Eve committed, led God to pronounce several curses as punishment to mankind in Genesis 3:16-20. One of those curses was upon the body of mankind. In Genesis 3:19, God said… *In the sweat of thy face shalt thou eat bread, till thou return unto the ground; for out of it wast thou taken: for dust thou art, and unto dust shalt thou return.*

Through this curse, our physical body was subjected to gradual degradation which is corruption till it returns to dust.

But God in his infinite mercy, made a promise to those who will inherit salvation. In 1 Corinthians 15:52-54, it says… *in an instant, in the twinkling of an eye, at the last trumpet. For the trumpet will sound, the dead will be raised imperishable, and we will be changed. For the perishable must be clothed with the imperishable, and the mortal with immortality. When the perishable has been clothed with the imperishable and the mortal with immortality, then the saying that is written will come to pass: "Death has been swallowed up in victory."*

These scripture are talking about the resurrection of the body. The old and corruptible body will be clothed with the imperishable body. This is the new body which we will don in eternity.

At resurrection, all the three components of Man; Spirit, Soul and body, will be reunited and the result will be a completely transformed and renewed man ready to inherit the promises of God in Eternity.

2.3 What does salvation give a man?

Salvation does not free you from your sinful nature. Upon his death on the cross, Jesus atoned or compensated for your sin. Though you are a sinner, Jesus gave you salvation which justifies you before God and gives you access to the seat of mercy so that God can hear and answer your prayer.

Salvation:
1. Justifies you – Justifies means (Just as if you had no sin)
   Romans 4:5 *However, to the one who does not work but trusts God who* **justifies** *the ungodly, their faith is credited as righteousness.*
2. Gives you access to the throne of God's mercy – to plead your case.
   John 14: 6 *Jesus answered, "I am the way and the truth and the life. No one comes to the Father except through me.*
3. Restores you to fellowship with God. 1 John 1:3 *"what we have seen and heard we proclaim to you also, so that you too may have fellowship with us; and indeed our fellowship is with the Father, and with His Son Jesus Christ."*
4. It gives a person the promise of eternal life and more so God is eager to answer the prayers of those who have accepted Christ Jesus - according to His will.
   1 John 5: 13-14 *I write these things to you who believe in the name of the Son of God so that you may know that you have eternal life. This is the confidence we have in approaching God: that if we ask anything according to his will, he hears us.*

Most important therefore, Salvation – brings acceptance before God and **sets the path** for you to be restored back to the former fellowship with God.

Let's look at the diagrammatic representation below to understand this restoration to fellowship with God.

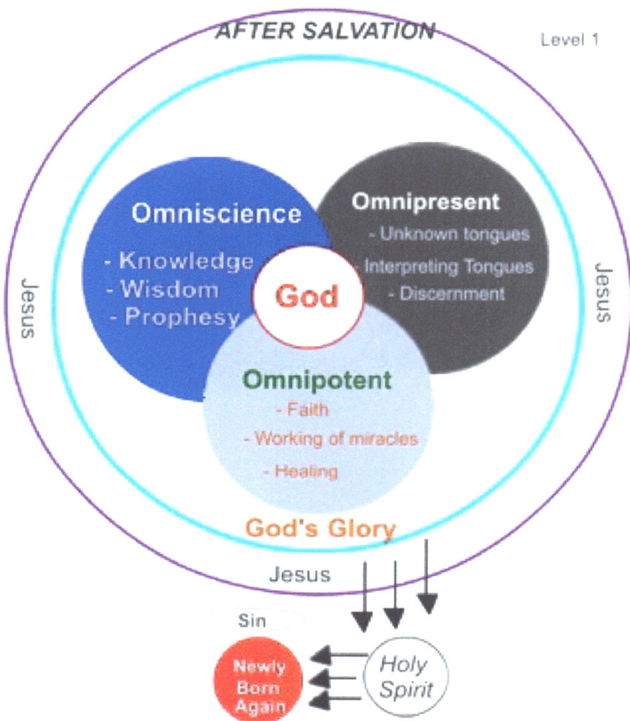

Notice here that Jesus comes into the picture. In John 14:6 *Jesus answered, "I am the way and the truth and the life. No one comes to the Father except through Me."*

Jesus is the only way to restore the former fellowship with God and to access God's Glory. Notice that I have deliberately labeled this level 1. This is the level that many newly born again Christians are. The Holy Spirit, the mediator, though available to them is still relatively unknown to them.

At this level, sin is always lurking at the door step of this Christian. He can easily fall (backslide). This Christian needs a lot of guidance into the word of God and love from those who are mature.

In John 14:15 - 20 Jesus Promises the Holy Spirit and says…

_15_ "If you love me, keep my commands. _16_ And I will ask the Father, and he will give you another advocate to help you and be with you forever — _17_ the Spirit of truth. The world cannot accept him, because it neither sees him nor knows him. But you know him, for he lives with you and will be in you. _18_ I will not leave you as orphans; I will come to you. _19_ Before long, the world will not see me anymore, but you will see me. Because I live, you also will live. _20_ On that day you will realize that I am in my Father, and you are in me, and I am in you._

The Holy Spirit (the advocate, the comforter, the helper) is the first link towards the restoration of fellowship with God. Being part of the trinity, He is the first that will come to the newly born again Christian.

The newly born again Christian is just like a new born baby. In the first few days, a new born baby cannot comprehend the mother yet they know she is there. When he breast feeds and begins to grow, the toddle slowly begins to grasp their surroundings and begins to learn the language of the parents. Soon the child becomes a toddler and is able to communicate with clear understanding with the parents.

The growth of a newly born again Christian follows a similar path. Here, however, it is your spirit that grows. It is the spirit that is born again and not the body. The spiritual food required to realize this growth is the word of God. There are three levels to spiritual feeding, or for feeding on the word of God.

1. Reading the word of God – The lowest level
2. Studying the word of God – a higher level than reading
3. Meditating on the word of God – the ultimate level to understanding the word of God.

All along, the Holy Spirit is available to help you. As your understanding of God's word increases, you begin to understand the languages of the spirit realm. These languages are:

1. Discernment
2. Speaking in tongues

A further explanation of these languages is given in section 2.3 (Languages of the Spirit realm)

Level 2 – Growth in the Knowledge of our Lord Jesus

The comprehension of the languages of the spirit realm is important and ushers you into the a higher level as a Christian which in this case I will call level 2 as depicted in the diagram below.

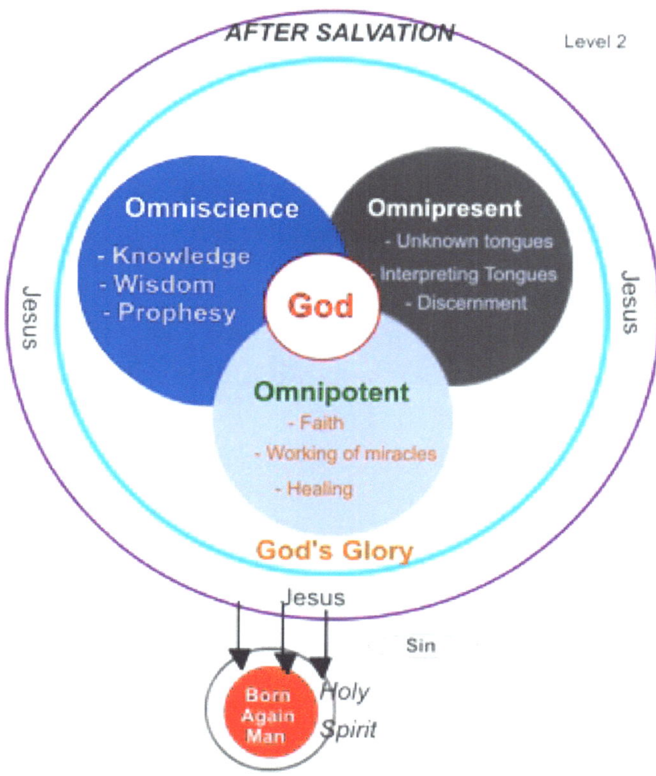

A Christian in this level is developing an elaborate relationship with the Holy Spirit as can be seen in the diagram. There is oneness between the Christian and the Holy Spirit. Notice that as the Christian grows to this level, sin seems to move further and further away because the Christian is more aware and takes steps to resist.

2 Peter 3: 17-18: _17_ *Therefore, beloved, since you already know these things, be on your guard not to be carried away by the error of the lawless and fall from your secure standing. _18_ But grow in the grace and knowledge of our Lord and Savior Jesus Christ. To Him be the glory both now and to the day of eternity. Amen.*

Level 3 – Christian Maturity

This is the ultimate level that you should yearn to be as a Christian. A Christian in this level has grown in the knowledge of our Lord Jesus Christ. The diagrammatic representation below depicts a high level of maturity in a Christian.

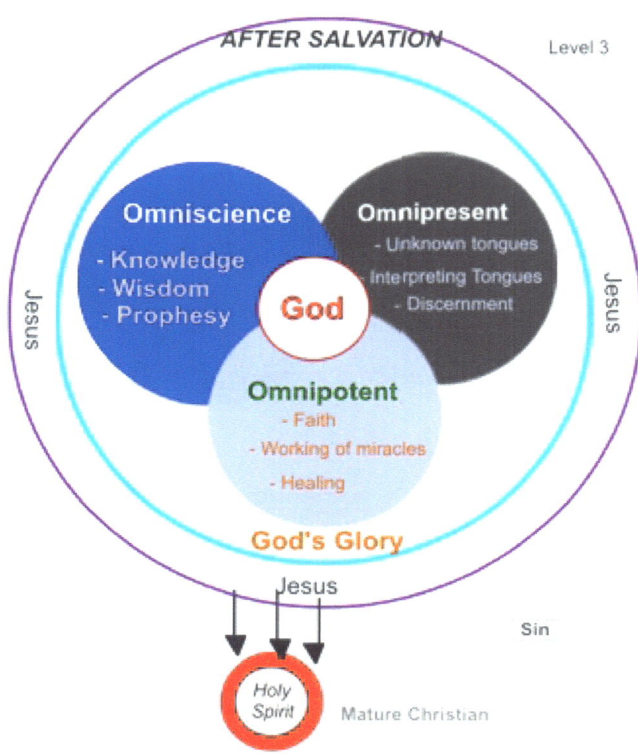

Notice that there is not only oneness with the Holy Spirit, but the Holy Spirit occupies the core of this person. The Holy Spirit is central in the life of this person. This is what is referred to as "being led by the Spirit". This person has yielded his/her self to the Spirit of God.

Galatians 5:18 says *"But if you are led by the Spirit, you are not under the Law."*

Romans 8:13-15 says *"For if you live according to the flesh, you will die; but if by the Spirit you put to death the deeds of the body, you will live. 14 For all who are led by the Spirit of God are sons of God. 15 For you did not receive a spirit of slavery that returns you to fear, but you received the Spirit of sonship, by whom we cry, "Abba! Father!"*

Salvation is supposed to restore us into full SONSHIP to God.

A mature Christian also manifests the fruits of the Spirit which are outlined in Galatians 5: 22- 23… *"But the fruit of the Spirit is love, joy, peace, longsuffering, kindness, goodness, faithfulness, meekness, self-control; against such there is no law."*

Question - In the light of all this, where are you at?

It is important to note that as you begin to grow into maturity as a Christian, the restoration starts by first increasing your understanding of the languages of the spirit realm. These languages are important to the restoration of the fellowship with God.

2.4 Languages of the Spirit Realm

In fellowshipping, there must be some form of communication that takes place - whether verbal on non-verbal and in a language that both of you understand.

The bible reveals to us three broad categories of tongues or languages: These are:

1. The tongues of Men (1 Corinthians 13: 1)
2. The Tongues of Angels (1 Corinthians 13: 1)
3. The Unknown tongues (1 Corinthians 14: 2)

English, Mandarin, German, Kiswahili etc. are called tongues of men and are all verbal. Tongues of men are primarily spoken in the physical realm. The physical realm is comprised of the earth and all the space we see with our physical eyes and the Spirit Realm comprises the heavens and all that we cannot see with our physical eyes.

Angelic tongues and unknown tongues are spoken in the spiritual realm.

Angelic Tongues

An example of Angelic tongues can be seen in Revelation chapter 4. In verse 1, Apostle John says… *"After this I looked, and, behold, a door was opened in heaven: and the first voice which I heard was as it were of **a trumpet talking with me***; which said, Come up hither, and I will shew thee things which must be hereafter."*

Though John was physically present in the world, he was ushered into the spiritual realm when his spiritual eyes were opened and the voice he heard was like a trumpet talking to him.

Because he was a man, he could only relate the sound of the voice talking to him to a trumpet. In the heavens, the voice of an angel speaking may sound to a man as a trumpet.

Another instance of an angelic tongue is recorded in Daniel 10: 4 -7. Though there were other people with him, only Daniel saw the angel (verse 7) meaning that only his spiritual eyes were opened.

In verse 6 Daniel says of the angel… *His body also was like the beryl, and his face as the appearance of lightning, and his eyes as lamps of fire, and his arms and his feet like in colour to polished brass, and **the voice of his words like the voice of a multitude***.

When the angel spoke, Daniel could only relate his voice to the voices of many people speaking at once.

Unknown Tongues

1 Corinthians 14: 2 …*For he that speaketh in an **unknown tongue** speaketh not unto men, but unto God: for no man understandeth him; howbeit in the spirit he speaketh mysteries.*

Speaking in unknown tongues is not the same as speaking in tongues. Speaking in tongues is a gift given to man by the Holy Spirit which enables him to speak to men in a language or tongue of men he neither learned nor knows. (1 Corinthians 12: 9) An example of this happened during the day of the Pentecost (Acts 2:1-12)

On the other hand, speaking in unknown tongues is speaking directly to God. This is also enabled by the Holy Spirit. Romans 8:26 says... *"In the same way, the Spirit helps us in our weakness. For we do not know how we ought to pray, but the Spirit Himself intercedes for us **with groans too deep for words.**"*

During prayer, the Holy Spirit can intercede for you with groaning and utterances too deep to understand. This is the unknown tongue that Paul was refereeing to in 1 Corinthians 14:2.

Angelic tongues and unknown tongues are not an everyday occurrence to a man. The third language, which is the most commonly used to communicate in the spirit realm, is DISCERNMENT.

Discernment

Again, Discernment is a gift of the Holy Spirit (1 Corinthians 12:9). Discernment is a non-verbal language and is what the spirit of man uses to communicate in the spirit realm on an ongoing basis.

To be spirit led, is to be able to discern what the spirit of God is saying about something or a situation. Discernment is, understanding something without being spoken to. It is listening to an inner voice that tells you what to do about something or a situation. You can even catch yourself nodding your head or saying yes or no under your breath when you are alone.

Our spirit communicates through the language of discernment. However, if you have not developed an elaborate relationship with the Holy Spirit to the level of understanding when He says something, God has another way of speaking to you.

When you go into sleep, it is only the body that sleeps. The spirit of man never sleeps and keeps on wandering here and there. As it wanders, it sees and experiences things. This is what we call dreams.

In the state of sleep, a man's spirit can receive instructions from God for the purposes of warning him or giving him directions.

Job 33:14-15 gives us an insight of this: *14 For God does speak—now one way, now another—though no one perceives it. 15 In a dream, in a vision of the night, when deep sleep falls on people as they slumber in their beds, 16 he may speak in their ears and terrify them with warnings, 17 to turn them from wrongdoing and keep them from pride, 18 to preserve them from the pit, their lives from perishing by the sword.*

Because God is Spirit, He can reach out and communicate to our spirit when our body sleeps. The body (also called flesh) is the biggest barrier to hearing God. Therefore God waits for the body to get out of the way when you go to sleep before he talks to you…to warn you…to turn you from wrong doing so as to preserve you.

When you wake up, you marvel at the dream and seek to interpret what it means. You must develop a habit of recording your most profound dreams because there in, could be an instruction that you cannot afford to ignore.

Discernment is the only language that can give you interpretation for your dreams.

If you have never asked God in your prayers to give you the gift of discernment, then stop everything else NOW! And go on your Knees and ask him to give you this gift.

What will Discernment help you with?

1. You will gain deeper understanding of the word of God,
2. You will be able to tell truth from lies,
3. You will be able to tell a man of God and a Phony,

4. You will begin to understand what God wants you to do,

5. You begin to understand what God wants you to pray for etc.

The gift of discernment is the KEY to unlocking what salvation affords to you. Without it, you will not be able to be established in your salvation. You will be tossed around by every false doctrine around you.

Summary

- Salvation is receiving acceptance into the Kingdom of God.
- Salvation is supposed to remove the language barrier that keeps you from hearing what God is saying about your situation.
- Salvation is the restoration of the former fellowship with God for the purposes of knowing God's will or purpose for your life.

In God's kingdom, there is work to be done. Our God is a working God and He expect us to also work. He has a special purpose for each one of us in His kingdom, but he can only work with those who can hear Him when He speaks so that He can give them instruction.

Salvation is work. It is the beginning of being ushered into a working Kingdom. In Philippians 2:12 Paul says… *"Therefore, my beloved, just as you have always obeyed, not only in my presence, but now even more in my absence, continue to work out your salvation with fear and trembling."*

Working out your salvation means that Salvation is not a fire escape from hell, but rather a call to know and fulfill your purpose.

In the next section, you will begin to appreciate salvation as the door to the revealing and fulfilling your purpose.

CHAPTER 3

Salvation & Purpose

The essence of salvation is to be restored back into fellowship with God and then to receive revelation on your purpose in His kingdom. He can only do this when you accept His invitation to enter into fellowship with him. When this fellowship with God is restored and your purpose is revealed, you begin to receive direction.

Your journey to discovering and fulfilling your purpose begins with salvation, followed by the restoration to fellowship with God.

This is the only sure way of enjoying the fruits of salvation.

In Matthew 28:19 Jesus commanded his disciples… *Therefore go and make disciples of all nations, baptizing them in the name of the Father, and of the Son, and of the Holy Spirit.*

Disciples are Christians who know their purpose and are busy going about fulfilling it. Jesus did not command his disciples… *Therefore go and make church members of all nations…*

Today, Churches are busy fishing for members instead of following on the great commission to go and make disciples (Christians who know their purpose).

God's Kingdom's biggest challenge today is church members…people who do not know their purpose. Once you know your purpose, your focus shifts to fulfilling your mandate.

A Christian, who does not know his or her purpose, can easily become a busy body in the church. Busy bodies are dangerous because when they do not find something to do, they end up becoming: Gossipers, slanderers, critical of others, self-righteous, judgmental, non-accommodating, lovers of themselves and the list goes on.

The question is this…from where you stand, are you a church member or a disciple of Jesus?

3.1: Discipleship is Your Purpose
What is purpose? It is the reason why you exist. When you discover the reason why you exist, everything else in your life becomes secondary.

Why is discipleship your purpose?

First a disciple is a follower, one who accepts and assists in spreading the doctrines and good news of the gospel of Jesus Christ. Christian discipleship is the process by which disciples grow in the knowledge of our Lord Jesus Christ and are equipped by the Holy Spirit, who dwells in our hearts, to accomplish this task.

Whether you are a doctor, an engineer, a teacher, a social worker, a business person or a student, you have a part to play in spreading the gospel of Christ. When God reveals to you your purpose, he starts guiding you on how to fulfill it regardless of your profession. The **how** is what differs from one Christian to another. The Holy Spirit is supposed to equip you with the gifts you need to fulfill your mandate.

Let's look at the story of the young ruler in Mark 10: 17 – 22 to draw some understanding about discipleship.

17 And when he was gone forth into the way, there came one running, and kneeled to him, and asked him, Good Master, what shall I do that I may inherit eternal life?
18 And Jesus said unto him, Why callest thou me good? there is none good but one, that is, God. 19 Thou knowest the commandments, Do not commit adultery, Do not kill, Do not steal, Do not bear false witness, Defraud not, Honour thy father and mother.
20 And he answered and said unto him, Master, all these have I observed from my youth.
*21 Then Jesus beholding him **loved him**, and said unto him, One thing thou lackest: go thy way, sell whatsoever thou hast, and give to the poor, and thou shalt have treasure in heaven: and come, take up the cross, and follow me.*
22 And he was sad at that saying, and went away grieved: for he had great possessions.

As we had established earlier, the essence of salvation is to restore fellowship with God. Restoration of our fellowship with God is progressive. During this restoration, we learn how to love God. You cannot be friends or enter into companionship with someone whom you do not love. Therefore love is the highest expression of our fellowship with God.

Jesus says in John 14: 21 that *"**Whoever has my commands and keeps them is the one who loves me**. The one who loves me will be loved by my Father, and I too will love them and show myself to them."*

Jesus says here that the direct measure of your love for him is through obedience to his commandments. The young ruler in Mark 10: 17 – 22 fulfilled this requirement when he says in verse 20… *"all these have I observed from my youth"*.

Then something amazing happens in the next verse…**Jesus Loved him** and looked right through him and saw what was going to prevent the young ruler from following him (becoming his disciple). It was his possessions. The young man had idolized what he had as possessions. When Jesus pointed this out, the young man who came running to Jesus walked away full of sorrow.

When you begin working on the restoration of your fellowship with God, He will begin to point out to you the idols that will keep you from fulfilling your purpose.

What do you think would have happened if the young ruler had agreed to sell his possessions? Possibly - a double restoration. Job received a double restoration when he remained faithful to God after everything had been taken away from him (Job 42: 10).

Mathew 6:33 is always beckoning us to seek first the kingdom of God, and his righteousness; and all these things shall be added unto you.

When your purpose is revealed to you, your priorities shift. You become more aware of the goal which is to fulfill your purpose than your needs. This is what seeking the kingdom of God all is about.

Therefore your role is to discover your purpose in discipleship. You can choose to remain a church member or you can decide today to become a disciple of Christ. If you make it your priority today to find your purpose, God will help you fulfill it.

3.2: Fulfilling your Purpose

As I write this book, I am continuing to fulfill my purpose. I started writing way back in 2004 and my first compilation was a book titled "How to Write a Winning CV". Little did I know then that one day, 10 years later, that God would reveal to me His purpose for me in an encounter during a 3 days prayer and fasting retreat. Afterwards, I compiled my First Christian book titled "Goal Setting for Todays Christian".

When God reveals to your purpose, you begin to understand things at a higher level. The Holy Spirit gives you gifts that will propel you towards excellence in fulfilling your purpose.

All along, Satan, who is referred variously as your adversary, is actually a tool in God's hands to test your commitment and help you remain on course.

Satan, being very cunning will try to derail or disrupt you from attaining your goal. He will bring counterfeits to distract you; he will attack you, he will attack your loved ones, but either way… James 4:7 gives you the best advice…to **submit yourselves therefore to God**. *Resist the devil, and he will flee from you.*

Submitting yourself to God means to do all that you can to remain in fellowship with him regardless of the challenges that come your way. As you do this, you begin to earn God's trust. You become a good friend to him like Abraham did. And He will not withhold from you anything that he is about to do. You become a beloved friend.

3.3: Becoming the beloved of God

Never lose your focus. When you have come this far with God and you are on the right path, he will not only love you, but you become a beloved servant like Daniel (Daniel 10:11, 19) and He will boast about you like he did with Job (Job 1:8 and Job 2:3).

When you become beloved or when God boasts about you, you will not be free of trials and tribulations. In Romans 5: 3-4 Paul says:

3 Not only so, but we also glory in our sufferings, because we know that suffering produces perseverance; 4 perseverance, character; and character, hope. 5 And hope does not put us to shame, because God's love has been poured out into our hearts through the Holy Spirit, who has been given to us.

When you are fulfilling your purpose, there will be an outward working of love in your life. You will be so engrossed that you will be able to glory in suffering as Paul says in verse 3. Your focus will be total. You will love others despite them withholding love from you.

The buildup of this outworking of love is a culmination of 2 Peter 1: 5 -8:

*5 For this very reason, make every effort to add to your **faith** goodness; and to **goodness, knowledge**; 6 and to knowledge, **self-control**; and to self-control, **perseverance**; and to perseverance, **godliness**; 7 and to godliness, **mutual affection**; and to mutual affection, **love**. 8 For if you possess these qualities in increasing measure, they will keep you from being ineffective and unproductive in your knowledge of our Lord Jesus Christ.*

This scripture shows us an up-building of a Christian's character whose climax is love.

- The first level is Faith: Total trust in God.
- The second level is goodness or diligence: Excellence in what you do.
- Third level is Knowledge: You receive revelations
- Fourth Level is self-control: Not everything is beneficial
- Fifth level is Godliness: God goes with you wherever you go.
- Sixth level is Mutual love: This is brotherly love or kindness
- Seventh level is love: The ultimate Goal of Christian living is to LOVE.

This is a love that loves those who wrong or persecute you. This is the pinnacle of salvation in a Christian's life and the restoration of God's Glory in your life.

The process of fulfilling of your purpose is the beginning of the manifestation of God's Glory in your life.

The following flow chart represents the cyclic process that sums up the restoration of the former Glory of God in your life.

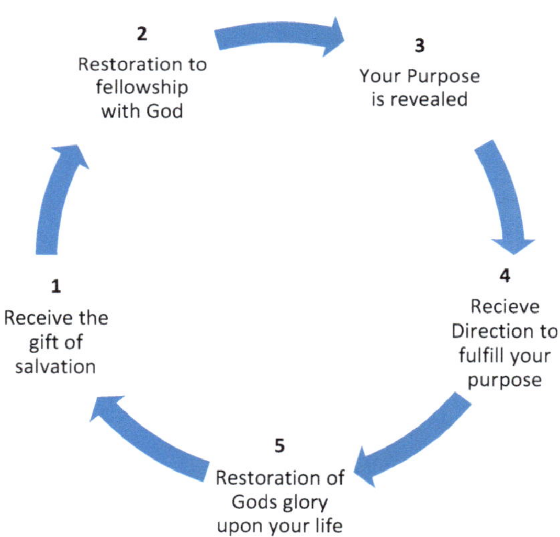

1. You receive the gift of salvation – acceptance into the Kingdom
2. You embark on the restoration of the former fellowship with God - Restoration
3. You receive revelation for your role in His Kingdom – Your Purpose
4. You receive direction – Fulfilling your purpose

5.   Restoration of God's Glory upon your life – Receive eternal joy

These above steps highlight the completeness of a man's salvation.

Summary

Every Kingdom has similar structures made up of: The King, Princes, Council of elders and servants of different stature and caliber. All these perform various duties for the kingdom to be able to function properly.

When a kingdom admits you, the first thing you do is to acquaint yourself with the language of the people of that kingdom. When you understand the language, you begin to gain deeper understanding of how the kingdom functions. You easily find your place and purpose in the kingdom. In other words you become useful. When you work diligently and excel in your purpose, the king will notice and might elevate you to even sit in the council of elders.

God's kingdom shares these similarities. Many Christians today, who have received admission into the Kingdom of God through salvation, are yet to know the language of the Kingdom and have therefore not found their place in the kingdom. They are yet to find their place and function in the Kingdom. Even though they have been admitted into the Kingdom, they are still strangers. Are you saved and still a stranger in God's kingdom?

CHAPTER 4

CONCLUSION

"Saved by a stranger"

You are in a lake drowning. A stranger comes to your rescue and pulls you out. He takes you to his home and gives you a change of clothes and a warm meal and tells you, "let's be friends from now on…here is my number… you can call on me anytime you want."

But when you leave, you never go back or call!

Many Christians can attest to this story. After receiving the gift of salvation, they never go back or call on Jesus to start nurturing a relationship with Him and God.

What does a relationship with God affords you?

1. Access to privileged information (revelation) about the plans that God has for you – **all knowing!**
2. Favor in the eyes of both man and God. When you walk into a room, God walks in with you! Doors are opened for you and people willingly do things for you…**all Powerful!**
3. A shoulder to lean on and He gives you strength when you are facing tough moments and mountains in your life …**ever present!**

Do not let Jesus be a stranger in your life. He is has an outstretched hand of friendship towards you. Draw near to him. Search him and you will find him.

What Salvation isn't

Salvation is not a fire escape from hell, but rather a call to know your purpose. Anyone who wants to be saved because they are afraid of going to hell is motivated by the fear.

Romans 8: 15 says… *"For ye have not received the spirit of bondage again to fear; but ye have received the Spirit of adoption, whereby we cry, Abba, Father".*

The motive for your salvation should be love. 1 Peter 1:22-24 is the evidence that you have been born again.

22 Now that you have purified yourselves by obeying the truth so that you have sincere love for each other, love one another deeply, from the heart. 23 For you have been born again, not of perishable seed, but of imperishable, through the living and enduring word of God.

Love is the climax of a Christian's life!

How to contact The Lord My Glory Ministries:
- For general enquiries write to: info@lordmyglory.org
- To support the ministry in publishing this free book:
    - call: +254 776 498 952 or
    - write to support@lordmyglory.org